Death

By W. W. Westcott

Copyright © 2021 Lamp of Trismegistus. All rights reserved. No part of this publication may be reproduced or transmitted in any form or by any means, electronic or mechanical, including photocopying, recording, or by any information storage and retrieval system, without permission in writing from Lamp of Trismegistus. Reviewers may quote brief passages.

ISBN: 978-1-63118-566-3

Esoteric Classics

Other Books in this Series and Related Titles

Aurora of the Philosophers by Paracelsus (978-1-63118-507-6)

Clairvoyance and Psychic Abilities by A Besant &c (978-1-63118-403-1)

The Feminine Occult by various authors (978-1-63118-711-7)

Rosicrucian Rules, Secret Signs, Codes and Symbols by various (978-1-63118-488-8)

An Outline of Theosophy by C W Leadbeater (978-1-63118-452-9)

Paracelsus, the Four Elements and Their Spirits by M P Hall (978-1-63118-400-0)

Essays on Ancient Magic by Helena P Blavatsky (978-1-63118-535-9)

Essays on the Esoteric Tradition of Karma by A Besant &c (978-1-63118-426-0)

The Use of Evil by Annie Besant (978-1-63118-532-8)

The Alchemical Catechism of Paracelsus by Paracelsus (978-1-63118-513-7)

Alchemy in the Nineteenth Century by Helena P Blavatsky (978-1-63118-446-8)

Qabbalistic Teachings and the Tree of Life by M P Hall (978-1-63118-482-6)

The Historic, Mythic and Mystic Christ by Annie Besant (978–1–63118–533–5)

The Hidden Mysteries of Christianity by Annie Besant (978–1–63118–534–2)

History, Analysis and Secret Tradition of the Tarot by Hall &c (978-1-63118-445-1)

Crystal Vision Through Crystal Gazing by Frater Achad (978-1-63118-455-0)

The Golden Verses of Pythagoras: Five Translations (978-1-63118-479-6)

Arcane Formulas or Mental Alchemy by W W Atkinson (978-1-63118-459-8)

The Machinery of the Mind by Dion Fortune (978-1-63118-451-2)

The A E Waite Reader: A Selection of Occult Essays (978-1-63118-515-1)

The Leadbeater Reader: A Selection of Occult Essays (978-1-63118-483-3)

Audio versions are also available on Audible, Amazon and Apple

Other Books in this Series and Related Titles

The Religion of Theosophy by Bhagwan Das (978–1–63118–565–6)

The Spirit of Zoroastrianism by Henry S Olcott (978–1–63118–564–9)

The Brotherhood of Religions by Annie Besant (978–1–63118–563–2)

Fourth Book of Maccabees by Josephus (978-1-63118-562-5)

The Story of Ahikar by Ahiqar (978-1-63118-561-8)

Vision of the Spirit by C. Jinarajadasa (978-1-63118-560-1)

Occult Arts by William Q. Judge (978-1-63118-559-5)

Kali the Mother by Sister Nivedita (978-1-63118-558-8)

Love and Death by Sri Aurobindo (978–1–63118–557–1)

Times and Seasons Volume 1, Numbers 4-6 (978-1-63118-556-4)

The Book of John Whitmer by John Whitmer (978-1-63118-554-0)

Interesting Account of Several Remarkable Visions (978-1-63118-553-3)

The Evening and Morning Star Volume 1, Numbers 11 & 12 (978-1-63118-552-6)

Private Diary of Joseph Smith 1832-1834 (978-1-63118-546-5)

An Address to All Believers in Christ Elder David Whitmer (978-1-63118-545-8)

A Manuscript on Far West by Reed Peck (978-1-63118-544-1)

The Story of Mormonism by James E Talmage (978-1-63118-543-4)

The Philosophy of Mormonism by James E Talmage (978-1-63118-542-7)

The Angel of the Prairie: or A Dream of the Future (978-1-63118-541-0)

The Book of Abraham: Mormon History by George Reynolds (978-1-63118-540-3)

Pearl of Great Price by Joseph Smith (978-1-63118-539-7)

Audio versions are also available on Audible, Amazon and Apple

Table of Contents

Introduction...7

Death by W. W. Westcott...9

Death by Eliphas Levi...29

INTRODUCTION

The word "esoteric" can be difficult to define. Esotericism in general can be seen less as a system of beliefs and more as a category, which encompasses numerous, different systems of beliefs. It's a bit of juxtaposition, since the word "esoteric" indicates something that few people know about, while the term itself broadly covers numerous philosophies, practices, areas of study and belief systems.

In a greater sense, Esotericism acts as a storehouse for secret knowledge, which is often considered ancient (by *tradition, if not by fact*), passed down from generation to generation, in private. At various times in history, simply possessing the knowledge of some of these subjects, was considered illegal and a jailable offence, if discovered. This usually included such general topics as Alchemy, Pharmacology, Qabalah, Hermeticism, Occultism, Ceremonial Magic, Astrology, Divination, Rosicrucianism and so on. Collectively, these areas of study were often referred to as the esoteric sciences.

Sometimes, the outer garment of a subject isn't esoteric, while what is hidden beneath it, is. As an example, Freemasonry isn't necessarily esoteric by nature (at *least not anymore*), but certain signs, passwords and handshakes given to the candidate during their initiation, are in fact, esoteric, in the sense that they are hidden from the general public.

Today, in the twenty-first century, such topics are readily available at bookstores across the country, and numerous mainsteam publishers offer beginners guides and coffee-table volumes on many of these subjects, intended for mass appeal. Books like *"The Secret"* have turned previously arcane topics into household knowledge. All that being the case, however, it isn't to say that there still aren't buried secrets to uncover, ancient wisdom being ignored and forgotten mysteries to be explored. In fact, it is often that we are only able to further our own studies by standing on the shoulders of these disappearing giants.

Lamp of Trismegistus is doing its part to help preserve humanity's esoteric history by making some of these classics available to those students who are seeking to unearth the knowledge of these ancient colossi.

So, be sure to check other titles from our *Esoteric Classics* series, as well as our *Occult Fiction, Theosophical Classics, Foundations of Freemasonry Series, Supernatural Fiction, Paranormal Research Series, Studies in Buddhism* and our *Christian Apocrypha Series*. You can also download the audio versions of most of these titles from Amazon, Apple or Audible, for learning on the go.

DEATH

By William Wynn Westcott

*delivered at the Adelphi T.S. Lodge
on February 6th, 1893*

"Death", according to the dictionary, is the "end of life", that is, the termination — not the aim — of life, in the common sense; and yet considering the universality of death among living beings, perhaps it is also the proper aim of life — to die — well. Still, it is not the whole of Death — to die, *i.e.,* for life to leave the body; we cannot safely omit to study the correlated changes, and new forms of existence which death sets in motion; whether it be the end of the life of a plant, or animal, or of a man.

The word *Death* is not only and always an absolute term, it is also used in a restricted sense; for not only may it be applied to the end of an entire organism, but also to one of its parts, and even to its molecules. In common language, the term Death is applied to the final change which occurs at the general cessation of the life of any body, animal or human; but this body is only the gross material casing, and but one temporary dwelling of the man. By "I", "thou" or "he", we *should* mean the "Thinker" which dwells in and inspires my, your or his body. Death is the severance of the Thinker from its dwelling, its clothing, its present suit of clothes; and in studying Death we may fitly glance at the subsequent stages of the history both of the Thinker who goes hence upon another stage of his long journey, and also at the fate of the soiled garments it throws aside. For the garments are soiled — by time, by use, and by abuse. Self-preservation is commonly said to be the first law of human nature, and setting aside the vagary of suicide, as apart from our present subject, it seems true that Death of the body only occurs when it is no longer physically avoidable. Death does not take place so long as the organism is perfect enough to form the dwelling of the vital force, and to confine the life essence.

Truly we ignorant mortals sometimes are amazed at facts actually observed; we wonder *how* some poor sick or injured patient lives so long; and at other times we wonder why some strong massive form is changed in a moment into mere earth. But we are mostly wise enough to believe that this wonder is but from want of knowledge; we know that there must have been a flaw there present, however deftly nature had hidden it. Medical science has already put its finger on many a *hidden flaw*, as the reason of death, but while it is a materialistic science, it will never discover the real flaws in every case. Science is an excellent thing, but science is yet a bigot, and she will lag behind the adept, so long as she is physical science alone, and neglects the "soul of things". Medical science has in regard to death made one very needful distinction, *viz.*, between molecular and somatic death: *i.e.*, between the death of tissue elements, atoms, or constituent parts, and Death of a whole animal being.

It is as natural to die as to be born, and the constant change, which is occurring in animal bodies, means constant birth and death of elements, of tissue atoms. Almost all tissues of living beings are of cellular construction, and each of the myriad of cells, visible under our microscopes, has a life and death independent of the death and life of the great creature into which it is built. The blood even is not alone a fluid, it contains millions of detached free living cells, each of which has a birth, life and death, and whose entire life history may only occupy a few hours, and bears no relation to the life of the man or animal.

Such then is molecular death. Somatic death — from the Greek word *soma*, the body — is the more or less sudden final change of the entire complex organism of a plant, animal or man. For a full explanation of all that medical science has learned of the somatic death of man, I must refer you to the textbooks of physiology and of medicine; but shortly may say, that the simplest classification of deaths is that from the primary failure of one of the great vital systems of internal organs; of these there are three, and so deaths are classed as from syncope, failure of the heart and circulatory system; asphyxia, failure of the respiratory organs; coma, failure of the brain, spinal cord and nervous system.

These may each be subdivided; for example, heart failures into — (a) sudden syncope; (b) asthenia, gradual weakening of cardiac force; (c) necraemia, gradual exhaustion from impurity of the blood; (d) from hemorrhage, sheer loss of blood, the vital circulating fluid.

But purely medical distinctions are not the subject to be dealt with in this lecture; rather is it desired to call attention to those other changes which death produces in man's constitution. It is proposed then to study the altered conditions of man's principles, which ensue upon the Death change, and to consider them from the point of view of the Theosophic constitution of mankind — with only a glance at the views of the Egyptian, Hebrew, Greek and Roman, and Christian cultus.

Almost universal in the ancient world was the doctrine of successive lives, of a series of earthly experiences. Reincarnation was the most general of all *post mortem* ideals, it was reserved for the religion which sprang up on the ruins of Roman civilization to popularize the dogma of a single life for each individual. It is very important to bear constantly in mind the fact, that the present views regarding *post mortem* states, and of an eternity of weal or woe, an alternative of never-ending reward or punishment, without further experience, are derived from the extensive spread of nominal Christianity, a doctrine which has reached its present development by a series of changes; at first by the acceptance of dogmas at the hands of dominant teachers who evolved them from their own sense of what was fitting, and later by successive concessions to public opinion and scientific investigation. Apart from parable and allegory, one cannot find in the words of Jesus any assertion of eternal Burning, or of everlasting white-robed choral service. The red-hot hell of the most orthodox European Christian, like the tailed and horned Satan, was evolved from the morbid fancies of bigot and priest in the dark ages of Europe. Eternity is truly said to be inconceivable, and as this is true, so is it true that no such period without change can exist. Longer than a life, longer than the life of a nation, longer than the life-history of a planetary world perhaps — but any stage of any existence, to be endless is a contradiction in terms, it indeed cannot be conceived, nor can it exist.

Death introduces a new order of things, new associations, new developments, but neither these, nor any further change will be infinite, so long as time exists or so far as time is conceivable — the human mind may indeed conceive of a spiritual plane, of spiritual persons beyond time and out of place — but in time — the idea of "changelessness" is an empty folly.

If I were asked, why Christianity has at once spread so widely, and at the same time why the civilization of Christian nations is so honeycombed with vice and hypocrisy, I should attribute as the reason, its dogma of a single life alone to each individual. Even today, after eighteen hundred years of Christian domination in Europe, it must be confessed that in Christian England, the purist of the world, the ratio of criminals to population is higher than in countries where the older great religions bear sway, and especially higher than in Buddhist and Brahmin lands, and higher than among either Hebrews or Mohammedans. Ancient Hebrews knew naught of immortality in joy, or in punishment, Rabbinic Judaism taught the doctrine of successive lives — so did the Mysteries of Ancient Egypt, so did the Greek aporrheta, and Roman cultus, and so did and so do the great Indian religions; and I believe the ideal of subsequent lives on earth — each tinctured by the conduct of the previous life, and each either hastening on or delaying a long and blissful reunion with the divine — tends more to a life of morality, purity and benevolence, than the ideal of an almost inconceivable eternal heaven, or the notion of a hell of eternal torment — inconsistent with the ideal of a benevolent Supreme Being.

In the Greek and Roman culture the notion of death was always softened, and the mention of it was avoided. Rather than say *he* died — *mortuus est;* they said *vixit* — he did live, or *fuit* — he was, but is not for a time. Sudden death was ascribed to Apollo or to Diana, respectively for a man or a woman; the former representing the sun, believed to have most concern and influence in a man's vitality, and the latter the moon, deemed to be most actively concerned in a woman's life. Compare the idea of the astrologic term, *hyleg,* meaning giver of life — it is *Sol* in a male *Natus,* and *Luna* in a female Natal figure. The classical nations used both sepulture and cremation for their dead, so that no general principle of their views on *post mortem* states can be gained from their funeral customs; with Egypt it is different, and their very ancient principle of embalming their dead has led the authorities to certain suggestions of doctrine.

That the ancient Egyptians believed in the return to earth of those who died, after a period of rest and temporary reward or punishment, is not only proved by modern researches into the meaning of the hieroglyphics that remain to us, but by the doctrine as related of the Egyptians by Herodotus, by Diogenes Laertius, Hecataeus, and by Aeneas Gazeus. Aulus Gellius notably refers to the same belief, giving as an example of one person reincarnating as another, the tradition that the soul of Pythagoras had previously been embodied in the form of a female named Alce. Ovid also gives narratives of rebirth. Much speculation has arisen as to the reason why the cultured and rich Egyptians spent so much time and money over the preservation of their dead, and the absurd reason, that it was because the soul when it returned would need or prefer its old body, has been adduced. Surely no persons would be so foolish as to prefer a worn and damaged shell to a new one that one can make very much what one pleases, or to almost any new one. Other suggestions have indeed been made, such as that they believed that the soul only lived as an independent spirit while the body was intact, or that the soul would only have another existence if the materials of the earlier body were intact from which to form the new body for the re-entering soul. To me, it seems a much more reasonable idea that the Egyptian preserved his father's body so as to preserve its shadow form — KHABA — the BA or shade of KHA — body, because they held as we do, that the astral form fades out with the body's decomposition, and the Kamic-rupa escapes also and becomes a prey to evil beings to ravage. It seems to me that he believed that preservation of the material body — the spiritual soul having risen — saved the principles of the lower man from suffering and from contamination by evil forces on the astral plane.

Theosophy gives us many suggestions and many sidelights upon the changes set up by Death, but even Theosophy cannot penetrate very far. There is indeed a veil drawn across the face of Nature in her doings with mortal men. But yet the T.S. teachings of *post mortem* states supplies a scheme which is eminently rational, even if incapable of demonstration, and is eminently satisfactory in its explanation of the varying fate and life-histories of the beings among whom we live, and whose interests should concern us as much as do our own personal hopes and fears, failures and successes. For distinctness, the fate of a man's several principles will be considered singly, after a short view of the death period.

It matters but little whether disease or accident has brought a man down to the valley of the shadow of death, at whose entrance we are now to meet him, and to trace his fate; whether he be in the home surrounded by friends or alone upon a desert, he must submit to the inevitable. If the death be sudden, the early stages are rapidly run through; and if the end be lingering the events of dissolution are all dwelt upon, and more fully realized.

By whichever path Death may approach the body, the cessation of the action of the three great vital centers rapidly occurs, one after, the other, regardless of which has been the first to fail. Death is, however, not an instantaneous change, as some have thought, and no physician, however skillful, can *in reality* name the moment of death. The life wave ebbs slowly out, and there are occasionally little wavelets of returning surge, whether of breathing, pulsation, or nervous muscular action. Let us accept the fate, and acknowledge that our brother is now dead — that somatic death is assured.

The once living, breathing, pulsating, thinking personality is no more; through what experiences has this thinker just passed, in the rapid transition from life and memory to the unknown shore?

Of one thing we may be assured, his physical sufferings

are at an end, the pains of disease and injured bodily organs have ceased to be appreciated by a brain whose center is devitalized. Brain and nerves work together, and die together, and the high entity of mind which has been seated there as on a throne, has left the tenement no longer suitable to its needs.

What are the pains of death? What can either orthodoxy or Theosophy do to alleviate them? Is dying painful? Or is it that the stage after death is painful? My contention is, that the body having reached that state in which life is no longer possible or capable of prolongation, it is the living, which is painful; it is the laborious struggles of the bruised and wounded organs to carry on their functions that cause the physical pain. It is the struggling muscles, spasm seized, by the exceptional stimuli they receive from brain centers, urging them to exertion to preserve the life that has become habitual; it is the passionate cry of the heart for more and purer blood supply, and it is the failing lungs, which panting with useless effort, supply the pangs of dissolution. It is the brain and nerves, slowly poisoned by the rapidly accumulating blood impurity that shriek in their semi-conscious existence, and which suffer in the common destruction. Such may the lingering death from disease be observed to be. Sudden destruction by accident, or syncope, saves one from these trials.

It is with the expiration and failure of mutual efforts of the organs to live, that peace arrives at last, and that death of the body is swallowed up, in victory over matter. Let us pray for a sudden death, if we would avoid physical suffering; let us hope for a speedy transition from health to dissolution to avoid bodily torture.

Thus far as to the physical pains of dying; but how of the mind, what are its experiences, which will be known by the adult. Of infants and those whose mental faculties have not expanded, we may suppose that the mind experiences are nil or but slight; but it is far otherwise with the man or woman who has passed a life of experiences, good and evil; of such as you and I, we must postulate a unique experience, and an awesome period of introspective trial.

From the earliest records of opinion, which have come down to us, and throughout the ages, there has been a general idea that the stage of Death is marked by a mental conception of the personal life history, by the perception of a panorama of past experiences. So general a consensus of opinion cannot be without foundation, and Theosophy accepts the accuracy of the popular dogma. As the death wave sweeps over a man we must believe that the death vision appears, and that a man appreciates his own conduct, and grasps the passing keys of his fleeting incarnation.

Backwards sweeps the vision from the awful present, back to yesterday, to last week, last month, last year, to a lost manhood, a transient boyhood, a dimmer childhood, and to an unknown origin. How terrible must such a retrospect be to most of us, more terrible still must the perception be, if it be that we view the life as from a point of vantage, and if we see the events in true succession, from effect to cause in grim reality, and deprived of the seeming and fallacious reasonings and motives by which we in past life glossed over deed after deed, and failure after failure, fault after fault, lack of charity after lack of zeal. May it be granted unto us that this experience is but short, and that the failure of brain be simultaneous with failure of memory; we may well be thankful if it be that memory is brain function, and that when the Manas escapes from its material environment, all earthly incidents fade out and only the higher and spiritual attainments are thereafter realized and carried on to the next step of the ladder. Let us hope that the lower principles, escaping from the corpse, and cast off from the Manasic ray, may be senseless, and unconscious of life history, although we know they exist for some considerable period on another plane, and are tinctured and soiled by the events of a life, which, however earnest and good, must yet have provided them with many a stain and blemish.

Apart from this doctrine of a life review when at the point of death, the experience is rendered most probable by the fact that many persons in our own times, who have been brought down close to death by accidents, such as by drowning, by being stunned by blows, etc., have narrated a panoramic life vision of a partial character, extending back from the moment of injury to previous scenes of life, but never reaching the actual life origin. It may be that the moment of incarnation in vision coincides with the last moment of life; and hence no one who has returned from the confines of death, has reached the early stages of the life. I suggest, too that it may be that the onset of actual death is distinguished by the Manasic entity from the occurrence of the risk of death, and so that the vision is not only partial, but limited in quality and reality, and accuracy of self-realization. This seems the more probable from the fact that persons who have had this experience do not generally report upon the distress such a vision has caused them, which seems unreasonable, if the higher Manas be indeed perceiving at a glance the true facts and opinions of a life history.

I have some personal knowledge of this matter, for I have been thrown from a horse and stunned upon the roadway, and have felt the cessation of life history, the thud of the blow upon the head, followed by a notion of passing back from the blow to the ride, to the country passed through, to the home left an hour before, to the reason for leaving for the journey, and the previous day's events — then a void — then a sense of pain and the knowledge of returned earthly consciousness.

The occurrence of Death is the signal for a distribution of the human principles. The material body, which during life has been closely connected with the Linga Sharira, or astral form, the vehicle of Prana, or vitality, is slowly deserted by these. The astral escaping gradually from the flaccid body, and its departure with all the other principles leaves the material shell a prey to decomposition.

The body is a vast congeries of animate cells, and these again are composed of countless still more minute atoms, each a center of energy and impregnated with vital force. While this human form still retains the other principles which form it into a perfect whole, these living atoms are restrained into a certain course of existence, and are grouped into definite combinations for special purposes; but when the link is sundered, these countless "lives" are become a disorderly crowd, they run riot as powers of destruction and continuous disintegration, they become other forms repeatedly, each less stable than the last, until the human form, once the finest type of material development, is reduced to solid, fluids and gases of very simple constitution, even as the Hebrew said "the body shall return to dust as it was, when the Spirit does return to God who gave it" (*the word God here is Elohim, the noun Eloah=God, with feminine plural form, the seven great divine powers, who supply each a principle to man's constitution*).

The Linga Sharira as death becomes accomplished loosens its connection with the dying body, and gathers itself together from each organ and tissue which had been permeated by it, and then gradually escapes apparently from the region of the left side of the frame: oozing gradually forth it hovers like a cloud over the body, separating itself more and more, until but a thread of attachment remains, and at last the thread snaps, and the Linga bearing away the Pranic essence into the universal Jiva or Ocean of Life energy is definitely separated from the man who was. The Linga, formed like the material body of atoms, although of texture so fine as to be imperceptible to common men, meets the same fate, the atoms being gradually dissipated and distributed as the material atoms are dispersed.

Some persons who are clairvoyant can see the astral form escape at death, and are able to detect it hovering over a corpse long after separation has occurred; such clairvoyants are able under certain circumstances to perceive such phantom forms over recent graves, of cloudy texture impalpable, and sometimes of violet color, thus corroborating the Theosophic doctrine. The astral form is not entirely dissipated until the last stage of decomposition has been attained, and nothing remains but the bones, with which the Linga seems to have no relation.

The life of man, inhering in the astral form which preceded the physical body and upon which it was first molded, is but a drop of vitality from the ocean of life, and when death occurs the drop falls back into the ocean, and its identity is lost.

"The dewdrop slips into the shining sea", as Edwin Arnold has it in the concluding line of his "Light of Asia".

The fourth principle, the highest of the lower quaternary, is Kama, the animal soul; this has been also intimately in union with Prana, the vitality; the two together are the Nephesh of the Kabalist, the vital spark, which Genesis describes as the "breath of life" breathed into the early humanity, the first man, Adam, by the power, which originated him, then called "Jehovah Elohim", or the "Lord God".

This principle is the personality of beings lower than man, who are mindless; it is the will to live, the instinct of self-preservation, the animal passions, the sensual animality which prompts to food, drink and procreation. It is universally spread through the body of man, is the sentient agent, translating vibration into sensation. It has no independent vehicle during life, but when death occurs it accumulates around itself a *rupa* or form of astral matter, and lives for a time an independent existence, casting from it below the Linga Sharira, while the Manasic entity, or so much as is spiritual, escapes from it upward.

In ordinary mortals the Manasic ray from the upper triad, which has been for life linked with this Kamic, passional being, forfeits some portions of itself which have fallen from their high estate by sin and failure, and these at death are thrust forth from the purer Manas, which ascends to peace and temporary bliss in Devachan-Hades, and they are united by sad fate to Kama-rupa, thus enduing it with some consciousness, and rendering it a danger to humanity. The Kama-rupa of the perfect man would receive no contribution from the high Manas; it would be a brute, a shell, a senseless phantom, soon fading out, an elementary without evil influence. But the Kama-rupas of the wicked, and of suicides, although invisible to us men, are terrible realities, and sources of many dangers; they are the deluding spooks of the *séance* room, the dwellers on the threshold, to whom especially the unwary and untrained experimenter in magic exposes himself hence the risk of fooling with the occult arts.

These elementaries, the klippoth of the Kabalah, the shells of the dead, these fearful Kama-rupas or entities dwell on a *plane* contiguous to our own, but inappreciable to ordinary mortals. The Easterns call the plane Kama-loca, the place of the phantoms, but it is a state rather than a locality.

The pure and the wise need have no fear of these beings, and know, nothing of their existence; but men and women who are debauchees and live lives of crime and riot are at their mercy. Their evil aura attracts the denizens of Kama-loca; these rupas fix themselves on such fallen human beings and prompt them ever to greater excesses, and the last end of such is worse than the first.

Just a glance at the mysteries involving the fate of man's higher principles, and first of the human ego, Manas, the individuality, one of whose successive "falls into matter"; or "birth into life" forms the personal man, such as you and I are. The Immortal Manas sends out a ray of itself to incarnate in a human being, and to make a temporary dwelling in a form constituted of the lower quaternary. This Manasic ray is there allied for earth experience with the Kamic, living, self-protecting entity for a period of terrene existence, for weal or woe.

The life has been spent, and death has completed the stage of progress. The personality sheds, as has been described, its principles one by one, the body dropping dead and still, the Linga escaping and disintegrating, Prana re-becoming Jiva, and Kama cast aside to masquerade for a time on an astral plane. Then the highest principles close together, the Higher Manas draws back into its bosom all that is spiritually pure of the ray which has inspired the deceased to good works, and then passes into peace and rest for a time, into the blissful state of Devachan. This is the heaven of the Christians, but a state rather than a place, and has no finality within it; no rest in Devachan is eternal. Everlasting rest is not yet for the human Manas: life after life must be passed through race after race, and round after round of existence, before once more Pralaya falls upon active divine energy, or Manas becomes one with the Father in Heaven.

Of the two supreme essences of the Divine which have received names as related to man, I mean Atma, the seventh universal spirit, and of Buddhi, its vehicle, no man knows anything, nor can conceive of them, but as brooding over the Manasic principle and being its Heavenly Father and home, even as Genesis tells us that God brooded over the face of the waters of creation; these things are a mystery. I do not attempt any conception of the Divine: I stand in simple rapture at the contemplation of the One All.

Having completed then a rapid survey of the proximate fate of the several human principles, let us in conclusion look forward to securing a death of peace, by sustained efforts to do life's work worthily and well, so that the specter of our life, whom we must meet at its threshold, may but little distress us. The consciousness of a well spent life is a crown of reward; the last end of the man who has spent his days in selfish enjoyment and in sin, will indeed be haunted by the ghost of his sordid joys and his poisoned feasts. Let us strain every nerve to obey the moral law, and the precepts of mutual interdependence; such exertions have been recommended by every great teacher and philosopher and by the founders of every true religion; the precepts of the higher life have been universally commended by professors of every different faith — against such there is no law. The body is to be respected and preserved as long as possible; we are sent here to live, not to commit suicide; neglect of health is failure in life's mission; in life alone do we gain experience, do we make progress: on every stage experience has to be gained.

There is no progress in the grave whither thou goest; your intellectual entity is largely conditioned by its dwelling; be careful how you soil your home, this material temporary abode. Action and re-action are universal; you demean the body, you lower the mental faculties, and they are apt to lead the body in return still farther from the right path. As we sow, so shall we also reap; the night cometh — that is death — when no man can work.

The Devachanic interlude ensuing upon death may be a blissful rest, but it also is illusion, and leads to no progress, and in the next life we must take up the coil of life where we this time lay it down.

Let us work while it is yet day, let us cultivate length of days to obtain measure of progress — let us develop while we have the opportunity. But we are under Karmic law, which decides for us how long this present opportunity must last, within certain limits; we cannot anticipate the decision. We should work without personal ambition, as those who are ambitious; we should struggle upward, as those who fight for self, but we should fight for all; respect life as those do who desire life for its own sake: do these things and you will be as happy as those who live for happiness.

How excellent a thing it must be to spend a long life well, and to attain at last to death as the end of a long and arduous journey, to fall asleep in peace as from fatigue. For the aged, the final scene is often brief and the phenomena of dying imperceptible. At such a time the vivid recollections of a long life spent in benevolent self-sacrifice, in zealous endeavor to do the right, must constitute that *euthanasia* so much to be desired by all. Let us endeavor then so to live as to have no fear of death; holding such doctrines as I have described, to confess to a fear of death is to confess to an ill-spent life.

With many apologies, my friends, I conclude this lecture;

my feelings have led me astray into a moral disquisition, into a sermon which I have no right to preach to you; but whatever my failings, and they are many, I am zealous in my efforts to teach what little I know, of that which I believe to be true. Farewell.

DEATH

By Eliphas Levi
With Notes by Madame Blavatsky

Death is the necessary dissolution of imperfect combinations. It is the re-absorption of the rough outline of individual life into the great work of universal life; only the perfect is immortal.

It is a bath in oblivion. It is the fountain of youth where on one side plunges old age, and whence on the other issues infancy.[1]

Death is the transfiguration of the living; corpses are but the dead leaves of the Tree of Life which will still have all its leaves in the spring. The resurrection of men resembles eternally these leaves.

Perishable forms are conditioned by immortal types.

All who have lived upon earth, live there still in new exemplars of their types, but the souls which have surpassed their type receive elsewhere a new form based upon a more perfect type, as they mount ever on the ladder of worlds;[2] the

---

[1] Rebirth of the *Ego* after death, The Eastern, and especially Buddhistic doctrine of the evolution of the new, out of the old *Ego*.

[2] From one *loka* to the other: from a positive world of causes and activity, to a negative world of effects and passivity.

bad exemplars are broken, and their matter returned into the general mass.³

Our souls are as it were a music, of which our bodies are the instruments. The music exists without the instruments, but it cannot make itself heard without a material intermediary; the immaterial can neither be conceived nor grasped.

Man in his present existence only retains certain predispositions from his past existences.

Evocations of the dead are but condensations of memory, the imaginary coloration of the shades. To evoke those who are no longer there, is but to cause their types to re-issue from the imagination of nature.⁴

To be in direct communication with the imagination of nature, one must be either asleep, intoxicated, in an ecstacy, cataleptic, or mad.

---

³ Into Cosmic matter, when they necessarily lose their self-consciousness or individuality or are annihilated, as the Eastern Kabalists say.

⁴ To ardently desire to see a dead person is to *evoke* the images of that person, to call it forth from the astral light or ether wherein rest photographed the images of the *Past*. That is what is being partially done in the *seance-rooms*. The Spiritualists are unconscious NECROMANCERS.

The eternal memory preserves only the imperishable; all that passes in Time belongs of right to oblivion.

The preservation of corpses is a violation of the laws of nature; it is an outrage on the modesty of death, which hides the works of destruction, as we should hide those of reproduction. Preserving corpses is to create phantoms in the imagination of the earth;[5] the spectres of the night-mare, of hallucination, and fear, are but the wandering photographs of preserved corpses. It is these preserved or imperfectly destroyed corpses, which spread, amid the living, plague, cholera, contagious diseases, sadness, scepticism and disgust of life.[6] Death is exhaled by death. The cemeteries poison the atmosphere of towns, and the miasma of corpses blight the children even in the bosoms of their mothers.

Near Jerusalem in the Valley of Gehenna a perpetual fire was maintained for the combustion of filth and the carcasses of animals, and it is to this eternal fire that Jesus alluded when he says that the wicked shall be cast into *Gehenna*; signifying that dead souls will be treated as corpses.

The Talmud says that the souls of those who have not believed in immortality will not become immortal. It is faith

---

[5] To intensify these images in the astral or sidereal light.

[6] People begin intuitively to realize the great truth, and societies for burning bodies and *crematories* are now started in many places in Europe.

only which gives personal immortality;[7] science and reason can only affirm the general immortality.

The mortal sin is the suicide of the soul. This suicide would occur if the man devoted himself to evil with the full strength of his mind, with a perfect knowledge of good and evil, and an entire liberty of action which seems impossible in practice, but which is possible in theory, because the essence of an independent personality is an unconditioned liberty. The divinity imposes nothing upon man, not even existence. Man has a right to withdraw himself even from the divine goodness, and the dogma of eternal hell is only the assertion of eternal free-will.

God precipitates no one into hell. It is men who can go there freely, definitively and by their own choice.

Those who are in hell, that is to say, amid the gloom of evil[8] and the sufferings of the necessary punishment, without having absolutely so willed it, are called to emerge from it. This hell is for them only a purgatory. The damned completely, absolutely

---

[7] Faith and *will power*. Immortality is conditional, as we have ever stated. It is the reward of the pure and good. The wicked man, the material sensualist only survives. He who appreciates but physical pleasures will not and *cannot* live in the hereafter as a self-conscious Entity.

[8] That is to say, they are reborn in a "lower world" which is neither "Hell" nor any theological purgatory, but a world of nearly absolute *matter* and one preceding the last one in the "circle of necessity" from which "there is no redemption, for there reigns *absolute* spiritual darkness." (Book of Khiu-te.)

and without respite, is Satan who is not a rational existence, but a necessary hypothesis.

Satan is the last word of the creation. He is the end infinitely emancipated. He willed to be like God of which he is the opposite. God is the hypothesis necessary to reason, Satan the hypothesis necessary to unreason asserting itself as free-will.

To be immortal in good, one must identify oneself with God; to be immortal in evil, with Satan. These are the two poles of the world of souls; between these two poles vegetate and die without remembrance the useless portion of mankind.

Editor's Note.—This may seem incomprehensible to the average reader, for it is one of the most abstruse of the tenets of Occult doctrine. Nature is dual: there is a physical and material side, as there is a spiritual and moral side to it; and, there is both good and evil in it, the latter the necessary shadow to its light. To force oneself upon the current of immortality, or rather to secure for oneself an endless series of rebirths as conscious individualities—says the Book of Khiu-te Vol. XXXI, one must become a co-worker with nature, either for *good* or for *bad*, in her work of creation and reproduction, or in that of destruction. It is but the useless drones, which she gets rid of, violently ejecting and making them perish by the millions as self-conscious entities. Thus, while the good and the pure strive to reach *Nipang* (*nirvana* or that state of *absolute* existence and *absolute* consciousness—which, in the world of finite perceptions, is *non*-existence and *non*-

consciousness)—the wicked will seek, on the contrary, a series of lives as conscious, definite existences or beings, preferring to be ever suffering under the law of retributive justice rather than give up their lives as portions of the integral, universal whole. Being well aware that they can never hope to reach the final rest in pure spirit, or *nirvana*, they cling to life in any form, rather than give up that "desire for life," or *Tanha* which causes a new aggregation of *Skandas* or individuality to be reborn. Nature is as good a mother to the cruel bird of prey as she is to the harmless dove. Mother nature will punish her child, but since he has become her co-worker for destruction she cannot eject him. There are thoroughly wicked and depraved men, yet as highly intellectual and acutely *spiritual* for evil, as those who are spiritual for good. The *Egos* of these may escape the law of final destruction or annihilation for ages to come. That is what Éliphas Lévi means by becoming "immortal in evil," through identification with Satan. "I would thou wert *cold* or *hot*," says the vision of the *Revelation* to St. John (III. 15-16). "So then because thou art, *lukewarm* and neither cold nor hot, I will spue thee out of my mouth." The *Revelation* is an absolutely *Kabalistic* book. Heat and cold are the two "poles," *i.e.*, good and evil, *spirit* and *matter*. Nature *spues* the "lukewarm" or "the useless portion of mankind" out of her mouth, *i.e.*, annihilates them. This conception that a considerable portion of mankind may after all not have immortal souls, will not be new even to European readers. Coleridge himself likened the case to that of an oak tree bearing, indeed, millions of acorns, but acorns of which under normal conditions not one in a thousand ever developed into a tree, and suggested that as the majority of the acorns failed to develop into a new living tree, so possibly the majority of men fail to develop into a new living entity after this earthly death.

www.ingramcontent.com/pod-product-compliance
Lightning Source LLC
LaVergne TN
LVHW041503070426
835507LV00009B/787